Dark Poetic Musings

Dark
Poetic Musings

J.K. Brownridge

To My FAVOURITE Uncle! ENJOY!

Lots of love,

Jayne xxx

FIRST EDITION

Published in 2018 by
FeedARead.com Publishing – Arts Council funded

Photography by J.K Brownridge and Gord Donovan Powers.

Additional copies of this book may be purchased at
www.feedaread.com/books

This illustrated collection of dark poetry by J.K. Brownridge has been specially selected for those who can appreciate the mysterious side of human nature. Like the minor keys of stirring music, melancholy poetry can touch the soul in powerful ways. Emily Dickinson, Elizabeth Barrett Browning, Charlotte Bronte and so many other female poets have shown the way in their respected contributions. Perhaps this compilation can add something to the vast pool of sombre reflection.

Acknowledgements

I would like to thank, with all my heart, those who have helped me on this exciting and liberating journey. Thank you for helping make this book possible.

Gord Donovan Powers,
Jennie Jensen and
Rebecca Jane Menzies.
My wonderful photography models and inspiration.

Gord
for your support, encouragement and love.

My Parents
for your unwavering support, enthusiasm and love.

Thank you and much love to you all.

To
Keinan and Willow
my best creations

Contents

Introduction

It has been said that dark poetry is a place of sanctuary from the real world. There may be some truth to that, but perhaps the same could be said of any art form in that artistic endeavour seeks transportation to a world apart. Whether poetry, music, literature or painting, the objective of all art is to evoke emotional reaction.

But perhaps dark poems are unique in that they attempt to communicate thoughts and ideas that most people are afraid to express. Such poems deal with sad themes, but themes that are integral to the human condition, and topics that many people want to hear about. Certainly, this genre has been popular throughout history. Who can deny the dark essence of Edgar Allan Poe's poems and short stories? H.P. Lovecraft's macabre musings give readers a chilling account of the personal hardships he experienced, and Elizabeth Barrett Browning's physical and mental anguish is expressed in mournful clarity through her sombre poetry. Indeed, some of the best poems and stories of all time are sad, dark, haunting descriptions of suffering, despair and loss.

But why do we consider poetry in this genre to be dark? Historically, humans have always had a fascination with darkness. The world changes with the setting of the sun, and in prehistoric times, the ensuing darkness brought with it a fear of the hidden and the unknown. But it is from this fear that creativity found voice and expression. The inner darkness and pain of legendary poets was symbolically expressed in their poignant writings and poetry.

The dark poetry of today finds a variety of forms, but it is still dedicated to the expression of negative themes in a poetic manner. Post 1980s writers and poets hail from diverse backgrounds. Through modern media and communication, they seem to have tapped into the emotions of young people, especially women, in new and exciting ways. The internet has allowed sharing of creative works, including dark poetry, in ways that traditional artists could never have imagined.

Dark poetry is viewed by some as a medical purge, expressed in a synthesis of various emotions. Romance, broken hearts, sadness and loss are all common themes, deriving from music and fashion as well as from the ordinary experiences of life. When we consider the lyrics of traditional country music we can see that these themes are not so new. However, a peculiar dark twist introduced by punk rock bands in the 1980s seems to have influenced content and given license to greater structural freedom.

Poetic license has always been recognized and accepted, and this is clearly shown in the prose and poetry of all the great writers and artists. A metered, flowing style is normally expected. This is often modified for effect, of course, depending on the theme and individual style. Most poets make use of rhyming to some extent, though free verse is quite common as well.

While dark poetic content is a given, the poems in this book show a variety of structures. The selections are meant to be pondered and relished. Like all works of art, they succeed if they provoke emotional reaction. Enjoy.

Forward

Come with me if you would be so kind
Into the darkness of my mind;
Take my hand, there's nothing to fear;
Delve right in to all that is here.

Magick and mystery, sadness and woe
Madness and worry, come see it is so;
There can be no light without the dark,
Entwined forever never to part.

So come with me if you'd be so kind
into the darkness of my mind.

I

Cold

The Raven sits up in the tree
Cold, black eyes look down at me;
Does he know of Nevermore
And what became of dear Lenore?

Does he know of these strange things
And of the tale his creature sings?
Doomed forever to behold
The tale of Lenore that has been told.

I feel my fate shall soon come to pass,
Bound upon snow covered grass;
Trapped here alone and left to die,
Only to be watched by cold, black eyes.

II

The Walk

Come with me into the wood
Do not be scared, it does no good;
Take my hand I'll keep you close,
Keep you warm just like toast.

Trust me my dear I won't hurt you
Just like the others who've been here too.
They did not leave, they liked it here,
Could not leave me out of fear.

You'll meet them soon my lovely one,
Together we will all have fun;
Come with me into the wood,
And do not scream, it does no good.

III

Sweet Dreams

Now I lay me down in bed
To sleep the sleep of the dead;
Not to wake before break of day,
Then through the abyss where my demons play.

IV

Rebirth

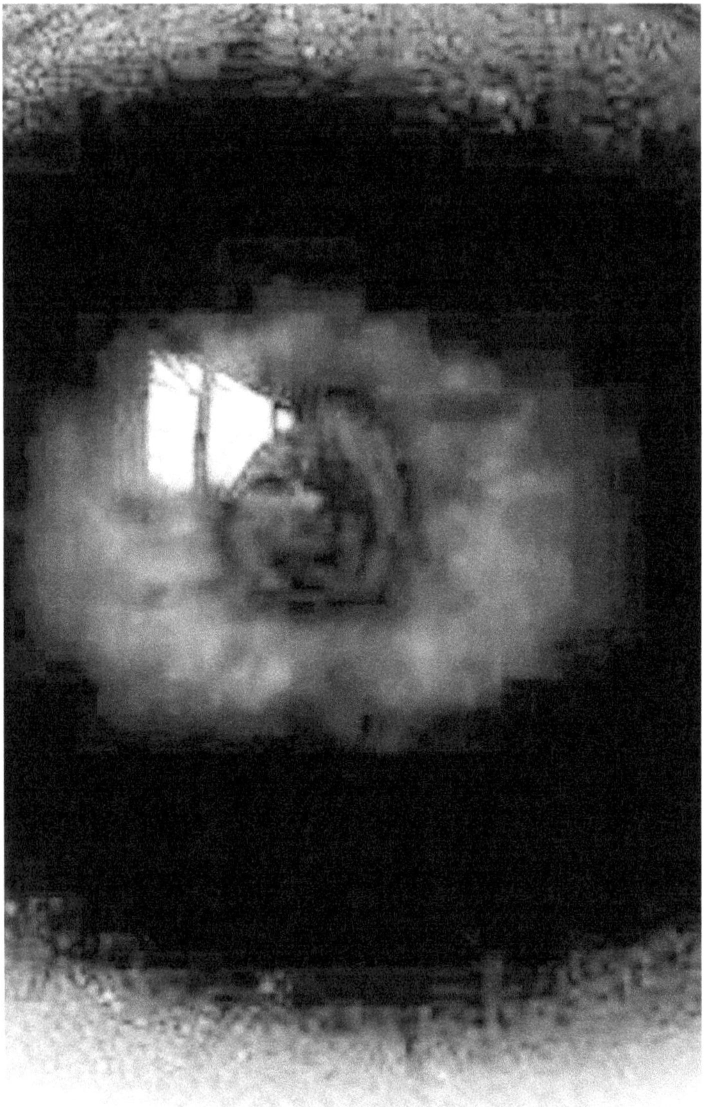

Little Demon in my head
You cannot have me, I'm not dead;
But when I'm cold and in the earth
Talk to me 'til my rebirth.

When I am to be reborn
In the darkness of the dawn,
Tell my soul of all your needs
So I may do your wicked deeds.

V

Part One

Wedding Day

She puts on the dress for her wedding day,
She couldn't know, she had no way;
For the one that she told no
Was waiting there, she didn't know.

The blade was long and it was sharp,
He gently pierced her tender heart;
The blood from her out did go
The life from her eyes so did flow.

With a beat still in her heart,
He whispered softly we will never part;
If I can't have you no one can,
The proof is in what I've just done.

VI

Part Two
Home

Welcome home my Angel
To your lovely home;
You will soon be feeling comfortable
Now the trouble is done.

Do not worry about feeling sad,
Those feelings soon shall pass;
This is now your new life,
The past is in the past.

Your eyes are soulless windows,
Your heart is empty, void of life;
Your skin so white and cold as glass,
But still you are my wife.

You tried to start your life anew,
But to me your life you gave;
The ground is black like Death's long cloak,
Your new home is your grave.

VII

Part Three

Funeral

The light shines brightly in my eyes
But I turn away with a heavy sigh;
I will go when my work is through
I must seek my vengeance on you.
You think you have won and have your prize;
It will come to you as a big surprise
To see me standing there once more,
And shake you to your very core;
You will pay the price for taking me;
You shall not live and never be free;
You must suffer as I have;
It is I who will have the last laugh.

I'm close behind you as you walk home,
Getting closer, we are alone;
I'm almost upon you, you sense me now,
You stop and slowly turn around.

The terrified scream that bursts from you
Has me delighted as you see me true;
A horrific grin upon my face,
Blood stained wedding dress I wear with grace.
You are rooted in terror to the ground,
I take my last step without a sound;
My blade is long and it is sharp,
I pierce it through your villainous heart.
A shrill cold laugh erupts from me,
Such a vicious sound of glee;
I am lifeless now as are you,
You did not win, I came back for you.

VIII

Waiting

I lie here defeated looking up to the trees;
My heart is heavy yet beats with ease;
I do not know how I got here,
Just that I'm lost and filled with fear.

I want to give up and finally let go,
Be happy and free from all sorrow;
I struggle and fight each blessed day,
I only want peace, there must be a way.

The earth is warm as is the sun,
She holds me close as if we're one;
She understands me like nothing else,
The only being that absolutely cares

I will stay here on my own,
In the earth my tears are sown;
Maybe this place will determine my fate
Until then I will simply wait.

IX

Sisters

sisters

Crimson red is the blood in her veins,
Flowing like water, burning like flames;
Standing under the full Blood Moon,
The time is near, the time is soon.

Pale cream skin and raven mane,
She calls out her Goddess name;
Her blood is racing, her heart it pounds,
She releases her soul into the ground.

An offering both pure and sweet,
Into Mother Earth beneath her feet;
The Moon is smiling upon the scene,
Her face is calm and most serene.

They embrace each other in the light,
Her spirit now has taken flight;
For they are one just as are we,
Sisters strong and Sisters free.

We are Sisters of the Moon;
We are Sisters of the Earth;
We are Sisters of the Flame;
We are Sisters from our Birth.

X

Guardian

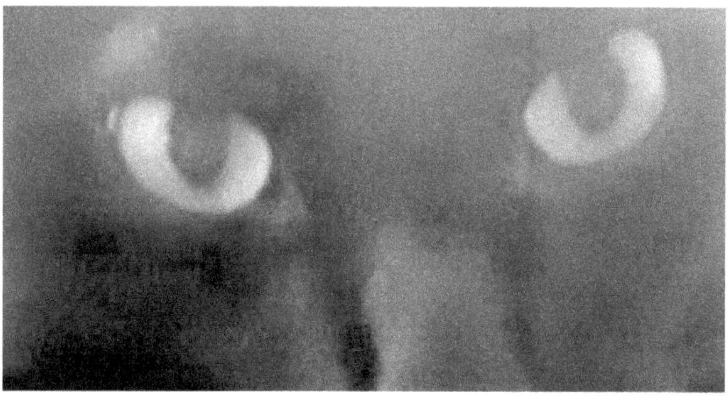

Eyes of emerald green so bright,
Coal black coat so sleek;
You pass between the realms with ease,
What is it that you seek?

Do you search for knowledge?
Or perhaps a spirit lost?
Like the summer flowers forgotten,
Underneath the frost.

Perhaps you keep my beasts at bay
When each night you fade away;
Over into darkness,
Eyes watchful on your prey.

Do you see my heart's desires,
My deepest secrets kept?
Whilst ever watching over me,
Your eyes lost in the depths.

I am honoured to care for you
As you watch over me;
You are mysterious and beautiful;
My protector you shall always be.

XI

Shattered

The night sky is silky black,
Not a star to be seen;
When the inky silence is shattered
By a ghastly piercing scream.

I frantically look around me,
Sat there in my bed,
Searching for that hideous sound
That fills me so with dread.

Now the dark desires are calling me
To fulfill their awful needs;
I cannot help but listen
And carry out their deeds.

I rise up from my bed of earth,
Cool as summer rain;
I do not wish to leave here
And be the cause of so much pain.

As I walk along the path well worn
I cannot help but weep,
For the ghastly scream that woke me,
You see, it came from me.

XII

Watched

You come into the woods at night
To find some solace here,
But little do you know
That someone watches there.

I've seen you many times before,
You are always on your own;
You think that you are safe here,
You could not be more wrong.

You look so lost and beautiful,
Delicate like a rose;
I can hardly contain my elation
To see your exquisite eyes close.

The forest provides me cover
To attend you unaware;
You will see me soon enough my lamb,
I'm so sorry you'll be scared.

I cannot help myself you see,
I've nothing here but time,
And wait for that splendid moment
When I make you mine.

I have let you come here undisturbed,
Now your time is at the end;
I'm coming for you now my dear
Into madness we'll descend.

XIII

My Pet

Come with me my love, my pet
On a stroll with me,
Together we can journey
Through life eternally.

Through dark halls dimly lit
The misty corners of my mind,
In rooms filled with treasures
And spaces free of time.

Do not be startled by the twilight
You will find in here so great;
It is only my Dark Mind my pet
Where I am able to create.

Join me in this dusky place
You and I, one for all time;
You are my love, you are my pet
Our Darkness is sublime.

XIV

One

We are bound to this earth for a time unknown;
We love and revere nature,
Feel a pull to be barefoot on the sandy beach,
In the lush forest and in flowing water.
Animals are drawn to us and we to them;
They trust us and know there is a connection of
our souls that forges our bond.
Magick comes naturally to us; we see it, feel it
And connect with it all around us in nature.

We can do amazing things with Magick
And we make it our own, all the while
Honouring what has been given to us
By Mother Earth.
The Moon and the Sun
Are our Goddess and God; we turn to them
For comfort, strength and guidance.
There is infinite wisdom in the phases of the
Moon and rising and setting of the Sun.

The elements of Air, Earth, Fire and Water
Are in our blood
As the wind in our hair, ground beneath our
feet, flames in our hearts
And the cool current in our veins.
We feel deeply for Mother Earth,
Connected as ONE.
We are bonded to each other in the same way,
Pledged together.

XV

Fire

Fire flickers
In the darkened space of the clearing;
The flames dance and swirl
In the soft summer breeze.

Above, the night birds sing a sweet song
As if delighted by the fire dance
That is playing out before them;
In the flames, much can be seen in the warm glow.

Watching the flames, in a trance,
Shapes take form; wings, leaves,
Animals of the forest and of the imagination
Take on shape and a life of their own.

The embers crackle, writhe and shift,
Inviting you into another world;
Although it is quiet and lonely here
There is company in this bonfire.

With the flames
You have warmth, comfort
And you are not alone.
Never alone.

XVI

Final Understanding

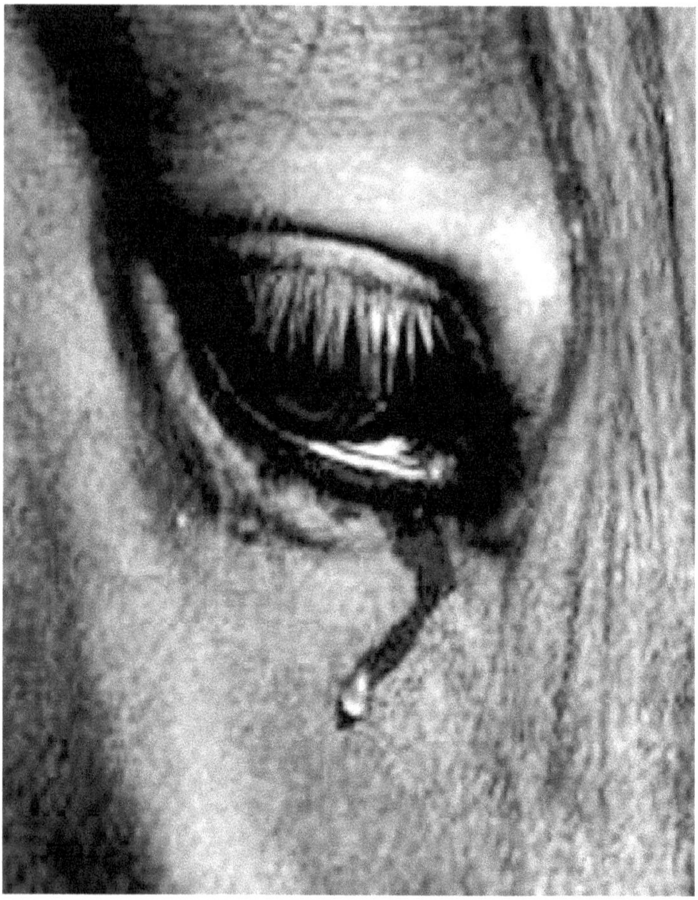

I watched her standing in the grass,
Her head low, her brown eyes so sad;
What happened to this mare?
How did she end up like this?
I only want to make it better for her.

Suddenly she knows I am there;
A furious spark lights up in her eyes,
She angrily whinnies
And tears away into the woods.

Months later, my heart in tatters,
My thoughts tumbling over each other
Like waves,
I return to the meadow;
The bay mare was not there, she was gone.

I did not think my heart could break any more,
But it did;
All my pent up emotions,
The tears, the sadness held deep in my soul
Flooded out like a dam had been burst open.

I lay down in the soft, green grass
And wept fiercely;
I did not care what became of me;
If life could be this cruel I wanted no part of it.

XVII

Final Understanding
(continued)

As I lay there, a warm breeze caressed my face;
A gentle, warm sensation touched my cheek;
I opened my eyes and looked up
Into the bay mare's face.

Her nose gently nuzzled my cheek again;
Her eyes looked into mine and in that moment
We truly understood each other's pain;
We both had broken hearts
And we both knew boundless sadness.

I stood up then
And wrapped my arms around her neck;
The bay mare rested her head
Against my shoulder.

We would be ok together,
Somehow we would move on
From this awful place,
And we would be happy again.

I had won her over with my despair;
She knew just how I felt;
You do understand don't you?
I whispered in her ear.
The bay mare gently whinnied in agreement.

XVIII

Drowning

I am the keeper of the pathway
To the world beyond this place;
Such sadness and such sorrow here
It will surely not be missed.
I watch and wait in silence
Only a wraith am I
Until the time is at hand
For these souls to say goodbye.
This lovely woman I see now
Is in such sweet lament;
She cannot stand to breathe this air
She begins her long descent.
She walks into the water
So cold and dark and deep;
She has had enough of living
Still it compels me so to weep.
She's drowned in life and living
This water is her peace;
What she has been looking for
That has been so out of reach.
When her misery is over
She wakes to see me there;
She is amazed she had another chance
As I smooth her matted hair.
I am here to guide you over
Earth never again you'll roam;
You will find new hope and happiness
My dear you are welcomed home.

XIX

Sorry

SORRY

Did you miss me?
No.
No?? Haha very funny.
I'm telling the truth.
I've been gone a week.
Yes, I know.
You're upsetting me.
Sorry.
I missed you.
Sorry.
I don't understand.
I know.
You don't love me anymore do you?
No.
I love you though.
I know.
What do I do now?
Leave.
Where should I go?
silence
But I love you.
Sorry.

XX

Dance of the Dead

Join with me in the dance of the Dead
There is nothing to fear and nothing to dread;
Together we waltz together we sway,
Entwined with each other that way we will stay.

Death is a journey much like is life,
We two as one in the depths of the night;
Dance with me for I'm at your command,
My beloved, let's away to that shadowy land.

XXI

Meet Me

Meet me under the moon
Meet me under the stars;
I don't care about your crimes
I don't care about your scars.

Your transgressions don't scare me
They are part of you;
Your flaws and your wounds
Are beautifully true.

The moonlit sky is waiting
For us to behold;
Into each other's arms
We will fold.

XXII

Tell Me

Tell me your worries,
Your sadness and woes;
Tell me your joys,
How your heart overflows.

Tell me your secrets
And thoughts unrevealed;
Tell me your story,
How you shall be healed.

Tell me your hopes,
Your desires great and small;
Tell me regardless
That I can see all.

XXIII

Glow

Candle flames flicker softly
Wide awake in the night,
Waiting for sleep to come
Watching the golden light.

Wax drips as a liquid snake
Following its path,
Gentle and soft it flows
Wrapping like a sash.

The flames are warm and glowing
Elegant and free;
I will watch and wait with patience
For sleep to come over me.

XXIV

Trapped

The ticking of the clock
Like the beating of my heart
Hammers in my head.
The drumming of my skin
In time with beat
Makes me want to shed it
Like a snake.

A fresh new skin,
A fresh new perspective;
Fire hot in my veins
Wanting to burn up
Like a Phoenix

And rise up new
From the ashes;
Soar to new views
From a great height;
I wish to see things differently.
Alas I am trapped as I am.

XXV

Save Me

The days are long and the nights are longer,
I'm growing weaker instead of stronger;
The light that once shone from me
Is now so dim I can barely see.

I can be saved if I let you in,
You will make the light glow strong again;
The price is great I will have to pay
I give you my will you will have your way.

My soul I will sell to live once more,
To see my life as I did before;
I am in your debt it is worth the pain,
Demon I'm yours, let me live again.

XXVI

Water

Water is unstoppable
It will never cease to flow;
No obstacle big or small
It finds its to place to go.

From the tiniest of streams
To oceans great and vast,
Bubbling brooks and rivers wide
Creeks slow and waterfalls fast.

Water rushes, trickles and cascades
Drowns, bursts and is swift;
Beautiful and peaceful
It is a treasure and a gift.

XXVII

Echoes

Echoes of the past live
As if they are broken pieces of glass
On the edges of my mind;
Sharp and dangerous
But I cannot see them clearly.

Only fragments come to me in dreams,
fleetingly in waking moments;
Trying to catch hold is like
Trying to grasp the winter wind
Or the morning mist.

There is menace
In these small shards of memory,
Perhaps best left unknown,
Yet they haunt me so;
Do I really want to relive
What might have been?

XXVIII

Five

Five sisters though not by blood
Brought together by fate;
They do not doubt they do not judge,
Bonded by Magick their strength is great.

Five sisters so together will stand
With each other no matter the day;
Power of Magick hand in hand,
Today, tomorrow, come what may.

Five sisters though not by blood
Will always have each one;
Force of Magick like a flood
They will not be undone.

XXIX

Red Rose

The red rose is beautiful,
Petals soft and smooth;
But be careful with the bloom
When you touch if you so choose.

The red rose has many thorns,
A warning sharp and fine,
A protection from harm and danger,
Take caution from the sign.

Prick your finger on the thorn
And scarlet drops come through,
Crimson as the petals soft
Pearls like morning dew.

Perhaps the rose is flaming
From others who have bled,
Ignoring the guardian thorns
Wanting just the flower instead.

XXX

Until Next Time

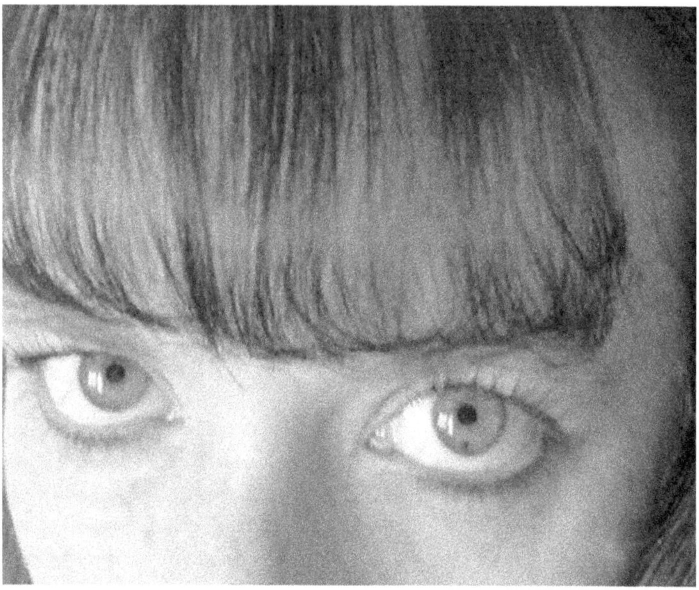

Here is where I leave you
Until we meet again;
It is not farewell or goodbye,
Just until the next time.

I am now in your heart
As you are in mine;
Always just a thought away
Our visit was sublime.

Did you enjoy your adventure
Here in my words?
Did they resonate, stir
Or perhaps open doors?

I'm thrilled that you joined me,
And you were so kind
To have come into the darkness,
The darkness of my mind.

About the Author

Jayne K. Brownridge is a Canadian artist and poet with an impressive range of diverse talent. As a registered reflexologist, natural health therapist, and group dance instructor, she has found unique and varied opportunities to apply her artistic expertise. This book of dark poetry is her most recent artistic creation.

Jayne lives in Bowmanville, Ontario, Canada.

CPSIA information can be obtained
at www.ICGtesting.com
Printed in the USA
LVHW111019261118
598263LV00001B/11/P

9 781788 765633